RUNAWAYS

**poems by
Lyle Crist**

1976
Pale Horse Press

Sketches by Rachel Crist

This collection is dedicated to my students; their own writings have enriched my view in significant ways.

L.M.C.

Second Printing, 1978

CONTENTS

awarenesses

WRITING

It begins as
a complaint,
a jarring inside;
persisting, these
incorrigible words
like runaways
push and shove
against the doors of my mind.

Once freed
they fall in lines
across pages
like troops marching.
I call out placements
in keyboard cadence
and watch their forms.

Words like runaways that push and shove
are but traces of a writer's love.

FOR DICK KINNEY

Neither sounds of children nor traces of the light;
gone the vibrant whispers, the melodies of being,
pictures of the day's bright seeing
in sensed patterns of the world. Delight
in all of these deprived. Lost each detail
of others, knowing scenes, sounds,; the paradigm
of expectations of life, unknown to him
who lives in vacuum's eternal veil.

Yet the star, not knowing darkness, still gleams;
in its own brilliance its world is infinite,
and love itself is unaware of opposite.
They persist for what they are, not what seems
and where they are, the want, the void
is not the vital stress
and where the mind persists, there is no less
than all to be discerned, enjoyed.

For him life's grand fruition overflows
in family, his school, his mission fraught
with touch and taste, remembered thought;
serenely he shares a life's rainbows.
No mourning! To sorrow's deep chagrin
judgment's message transcends all doubt:
it is not what he is without —
it is what he is, within.

FLOWER PEOPLE

In yard patches of city slopes —
ragged, green remnants of wilderness hopes—
mid belching chimneys; between these vaults
one finds in such desperate faults
that contrast persists and sometimes unfolds
in yellow and orange of wild marigolds.

How right each time that sorrow's chains
are severed by those who stake out claims
on something beyond this pitiful scene,
rooted, instead, in brief wisps of green.

So, one must make choices, and usually holds
to people who persist — like marigolds.

NOW AND ONCE

Almost antiseptic,
the garage this Saturday.
He moves in ordered paths, no need
for the broom, in place
against the wallboard,
its fringed comb
unwearing.

Saturdays once were taxing;
the kids' bikes, wagon, the
catcher's mitt and bat thrown.
It took half a day
to bring respectability
with hula hoops, wire coils
for rabbit hutch, the football,
pogo sticks, skates
in hurried heaps.

Hovering,
the muted neatness
and on the sheen of a recent shelf,
once playhouse siding,
his hand searches,
pulsing, like the
pendulum
of the clock on kitchen wall.

WATCHER

Redbirds come to the feeding station.
I keep grain there
and watch the bluejay, redbird, robin.
I stock it well
to assure the visits
and think of a time past when
my father looked at his birds
delighting in their calls
and the night he smiled and told me
he'd seen a wren.

I love them all and keep them fed.
I am a watcher of birds more than men,
looking at a redbird, bluejay, robin —
hoping for a wren.

ASPEN

Like
dangling earrings
from countless stem-lobes
the leaves frolic
on bouncing winds.

If my line of thought
is right,
the aspen
hears more
than any other
forest tree.

INTERRUPTIONS

Interruptions!
Why, you have
no idea
what they can mean
until
you
have observed
the tireless
crow
working away
at some remnant
in the right-hand lane
of Interstate 80.

LESSON

I am told that birds
stake out territories,
establish grassy areas of their own;
their songs from slender branches
more than mere tunes
so that "nothing inappropriate"
(a fieldguide phrase)
may enter here.

I must leave you now
applying what I've been taught —
to climb the
branches of my thought.

IT WAS LOVE

We called him Squirt, for
obvious reasons; yet the stray pup drew
steadily to me with wrestlings
and fetchings and other joys that grew.
I was 8 and off to school
he perched by walk as I said goodbye,
our home on the busy avenue.

Bounding back later on, I asked for him.
"Oh, some teachers — yes, two teachers — the pair
came by and asked if they might take him."
My mother's words. "They live where
a farm is big, with fields for him
to roam. They wanted to take him.
He will be much happier there."

I cursed the teachers for months; I accepted, yet
"Have them return him," I pleaded.
I had love for Squirt — what
more was ever needed?

One day, a generation later,
thinking of that house, once mine
I drove the avenue
three lanes, the horns, the tire whine,
past the site, and I thought
of Squirt and, as awareness can, the truth at last
illumined the whole design.

And I knew only that day — the loss.
My mother thought farm and field would separate
the truth, the kind you cannot
accept at all when you are 8.

I cursed again, now the cars that would
not stop, and wrestled my pup again, my
arms so full of him and of my mother's
hesitant words, her attempt awry.
But it was all love, of course. The pup, the words.
And the growing up. And looking out.
All to verify.

SUMMER STATUE

Alone
in layered July heat
that sears the mesa,
this horse has
no desert shrub
to shadow him.
Time of imperceptible motion
or, at most, muted cadence.

He has learned his lesson
and
statue-like
he stays
until the sky will deepen.
Even a blush will do.

THE SUDDEN UNEXPECTED

The sudden unexpected
lunges or sweeps at us,
jabs,
and occasionally touches the tip
of a nose
like a dusty moth
flying into somebody's business.
Damp, primordial swamps
loom,
even tears spill from lines to sheets,
heavy moist cloud layers
spill their water sacs,
sweat breaks and persists in wide covers.
Wetness is a hanging
and hovering.
But the dry—
unexpected.

PLACING CHRISTMAS WREATH ON DAD'S GRAVE

It is the silence,
the motionless sky
through gray strings
of hillside trees.
We place the wreath,
our brief evidence,
by the stone
then scuffle feet
against the leaves that died that fall,
years since the slow cadence into earth.
We clear throats,
I say a word,
anything. Mother nods,
then fusses with the green
and I pace again.

We will do all we can
in these scattered moments
to avoid the silence
that would, like burial itself,
mute thought
as it does
sight.

It is the silence
we despair.

ACADIA OCEANSIDE

No man can measure ocean pulse
that sounds upon the granite coast;
rebuke of ocean calculus
each perfect wave is nature's boast.

Numbered peaks speak to me
I count the sediment of time.
In joy I halt at ocean shore;
the throb of wave exceeds design.

THESE, BEYOND CHEMISTRY

These, beyond chemistry,
came high above a flat Indiana farm;
first as a TWA arrowhead reflecting the sun
it raced
across a deepless autumn sky.
I saw dual streaks,
trails of vapor condensation,
afterburner afterstreaks
dissipating in twin lanes, lingering,
and yet just as I would focus on them
they faded
and my gaze could not hold them.
Condensation, rarefaction, pressure,
temperature, front
were there detailing, defining.
Vacuum drawing wings upward, jets pushing.

But then, scanning my mind, I found
these other trails
that, too, disappear,
existing only for segments of time;
suspended moments in my mind beyond holding.
Childhood images, the games, early fears,
what love is, first hint of death.
My mind, too, races on, drawn, pushed.

These contrails of my mind —
beyond chemistry, these.

PROGRESS

His gills dilate, dilate.
Early morning swim and the black bass
hovers over watercress and algae clump,
finds friends have already nibbled, then
knifes downward going "oh-wa, oh-wa"
with his mouth tasting pond floor.

Dilate, dilate.

They sprayed the land around the pond last night,
marked the edges with browning cat tails so
supermart bulldozers could gouge the swamp;
but black bass, glides, not knowing
that man, too, nibbles.
And the poison rides the water crest.
unknown to him who hurtles through watery paths;
day life runs out on poisoned winds.

And soon they will not dilate, dilate.

PERSONALITY

The conversation was obvious,
a static thing,
and I wanted only
to rid myself
when

"Of course,"
this person said,
"there are answers.
What counts
is what prompts the questions:
mottled nightglow of leaves
against the street light,
a star seen but unknown,
and the toad unseen but known,
patience of tree rings enveloping,
and a paper clip resting
on a valued painting,
almost complimenting.
Have you thought of it that way?"

"No," I said,
"but
may I stay with you
a while more?"

IT IS THE KIND

Perhaps you have noticed
dogs in parked cars.
The toy poodles scurrying
around in Imperials, Cadillacs,
and
the shepherds, the Great Danes
in red Volkswagens and
yellow Volkswagens
so hunched, arched
in forced roofline fancy,
their paws splattering over seats
with hardly enough room
for the driver.

Of the two, I've found
more room for love
in the latter,
the jeaned drivers grinning commands,
then the ready conversation of
runs and forages,
the tussles and the hearty holds —
while the others, in velour
with no space to jump
go nowhere in common ground
with their masters.
There is only "now, now, now"
and "no, no, no."

You and I
would gladly hunch
for such acceptance as some have.
It is not the size or space.
It is the kind of love.

BEFORE THE DAWN

Before the dawn
the song began.
Before the sweep of light
— no matter if it was moments or more —
this backyard bird
sang, knowing;
his melody a harbinger.

And I thought
how often
only after rewards were given
have I sung;
but how
faith is a song

before the dawn.

encounters

WASHINGTON, D.C., FEBRUARY

Wind brittled cold
pushed through my coat
even to fingers huddled
within furred gloves.

I thought of how,
at worst,
it would be
if, without gloves,
I could only thrust
bare hands into the sleek
coat pockets.
Shuddering at the thought,
I saw a man
against the corner swirls
hunch, eyes slitted against
that wind,
and pole himself on.

He had neither left leg
nor gloves at all
and his fingers gritted
metal crutch bars.

BENSON HOTEL, PORTLAND

"You guys gotta see that
mirror in there!" The boy
had bounded over steps to the curb
past me (I was unimportant
in the contrast).
"Jeez! That mirror has gotta be
500 feet tall in there!"
His arm stretched to heaven, his
audience of 14-year-olds
responding.

Though faded jeans are modish,
theirs betrayed impoverished reality,
a genuineness that was
no part
of the high ceilinged hotel lobby.
They jabbered, and I on to the
lobby and room,
noticing now (I had passed it
a dozen times unthinking)
the mirror,
perhaps fifteen feet tall at landing.
For me it was no more.

For him at street edge, no credit card
check in, no TWA, no limousine, nor
expense account,
it was more.

Jeez! It had to be 500 feet!

INCIDENT DURING TOUR OF MALABAR FARM

"You can see on this wall
autographed copies
of many Hollywood personalities
who visited.
Humphrey Bogart was one.
Why, he and Loren Bacall
spent their honeymoon
right here! Right in this room!
They were Mr. Bromfield's guests.
This very furniture was used,
be careful how you touch, please.
Bogart was a frequent visitor
in other years, too.
Doesn't he look just grand in
this photograph!
And he used this very telephone
to call Hollywood!
He sat in *this* chair, mind you;
you can see the cushion wrinkles!
He was a favorite of the
children, too.
Are there any questions?"

"He's dead now, ain't he?"

"Yes."

INTERSECTIONS

He will not stop at red lights,
but intent upon being himself
and having the world know this
fact
he leaves behind
courthouse catacombs,
the statutes, dusty documents,
and turns, instead, to
leaping intersections,
jaywalking the Volkswagen;
bolting past the
light which blinks
in disbelief.

The car wears its bruises well,
mangled fender, pinched door,
under-plumbing askew from
crossroad buffeting.

But his lonely self,
the assertion,
the purposed ego,
is mostly untouched,
missed by all the crowd.

MY HIGH SCHOOL . . .

JUST BEFORE DEMOLITION

Three lockers, dimpled from years of kicks,
angled along the scarred wall, and
plaster peeled away in spots
like open sores along its corridor length.

Doors ajar told of classes no longer held,
broken chairs piled by the stairway,
lame desk straddling split threshold, a pennant
among debris in a corner.
This is too much! I said. Graves are not
to be splintered, opened! We do not
want corruption of what has been,
yet magnetism drew me to vacant rooms
once teeming; I began
retracing steps of another time,
my solitary walk before the crane-balls
smashed.

I was once here. These boards, now
warped with time, felt my touch
in study hall, my mind forming.
This blackboard, paunchy like my middle age,
I knew
and placed chalk across in equations.

And here in basement shop there was blood
by this lathe position, my fingers
pulsing.
College prep students were not adept at lathes;
careless, but no vestige now,

I studied my open hand, and I heard
myself in cold concrete room,
"Nothing from without,
nothing from within."

In here, room 209,
Richard sat, before he went off to a war
he wrote about in columns
in prophecies unknown.
What had been his thought in this room
when he argued Chaucer in honors class
before he crawled into a belly turret in Italy

and died in a B-17?
My God, was he actually a gunner?
His scholar's brains, wrinkling,
used on trajectories?

I lost myself then among 2,000 seats
in cavernous auditorium, hollow;
it was not made to be so silent
and curve of balcony seemed like
a mocking smile,
sideshow doorway, one walks from stage
into the face itself.
Turning, I saw them laughing, pouring in
for rally, gridders wearing emblems, books on
laps as we cheered, held tightly for alma mater.
And I heard myself on stage during
variety show, singing,
and above the gargoyle emblem stared down
as it had before.

I have walked the gaping corridors, long
length of my own thought,
probed paper scraps behind lockers
pushed from walls.
They have suffered enough kicks; their scars
to become deeper in crumpled scrap heaps
along some highway.
Within them we stored our lives.

Alone, I listen for today, but I hear only
the echo of my footsteps,
the distant wind tumbling through
a cracked window,
and the long, quiet anguish
of a memory, throbbing
in its own death throes.

SORRY, SAMSON

You *can* tell, of course.
He stands in line
at Eastern ticket counter, reading
the processed crowd,
his thin lips in
nervous motion,
the polished ebon
in perfect flow.
A helmet of (hair;
the clashing wisps
of sideburn gray.
You *can* tell, of course.

ON HAVING READ THE
PERFECT PAPER

Joy unbounded is mine today
I've given a theme a grade of A.
No participles dangled, no words misspelt.
It's the greatest joy I've ever felt!
Topic sentences, proper diction;
this sounds as though it must be fiction
but the words were there in right sequence.
Excellent expression! Some days hence
I'll put it back upon the shelf —
pretend I hadn't written it myself.

HONEYMOONERS
AT THE MOTEL

Arm in arm they go
their morning now the afterglow
of their celebration night.
I watch them stroll, this youthful sight.
Her levis are a pristine white,
in retrospect so very tight —
the pattern of her body mold
in lucid movement, delicious, bold.
One sees magnetic, supple lines
which by her clothes are more defined.
If she were in these arms of *mine*
I would — well, at any rate,
I, too, would celebrate.

LITERATURE PROF

The text had 187 short stories
and two cartons of poems
and a full index
(and there was something more than a
hundred pieces of asphalt tile on the
floor in the room; I started counting them
one day)
— as I said, there were 287
short stories and three cartons
of poems
or whatever the number was and
I spent most of my time
trying to show them what makes a story
click,
a poem
mean something
and I said, "See the cyclic effect in
this story by Trilling; a cycle of events
and we begin where we end and
we see the use of setting in 'Open Boat'
by Crane because the sea is unsafe and
land is security
and all four men must move from
danger to safety
and that is good use of setting.

And look at the richness of simple
reference in
Frost's 'Axe-Helve'. Imagine! A man
spending his life molding axe-helves!
But he knows there is a right helve for
each man and that, I submit,
is rich use of simple reference.
That is what I mean."
Pry open minds, wedge wisdom
so that they can see *for themselves* how it is
with literature.

Well, with 387 short stories and
four cartons of poems in our text
we finished, followed syllabus, and so
it was examination time and I asked
all that I could ask:
"From 487 short stories and five cartons
of poems, discuss use of cycle in stories,
tell me about useful setting, describe some
simple poetic reference that is rich
in universal meanings."

And paper and paper and paper and paper
came in for grading and they say,
"See! How well we know our lesson." They write,
 "See the cyclic effect in the Trilling story,
the cycle ends where it has begun and what
better setting could there be than land
and sea in 'Open Boat' for here
the sea is danger and land is safety;
how useful; how appropriate it is!"
They say, "And there is no better poetry of
simple reference than 'Ave-Helve' for
here is a man dedicated to molding an
axe-helve to the man, spending his life
to the proposition!"
And the papers summarize, "Truly this course
has given me wisdom and understanding and
awareness, for now I can discern what
literature is and I am much better for having
been in your class."

I am desolate,
but, with 587 short stories and six cartons
of poems in the text, nicely indexed,
I must meet another class next term.
Ah! I am afraid that soon I shall
do no more
than count the tiles
on the floor.

THE STORE

Mattel toys in neat stacks
along the discount aisles
bring a rush of cries;
little girls pick up dolls
and boys go rat-a-tat
and push trucks unashamed
in front of me
and discovery shouts
echo as I look
in muted glances for
this day's necessary item
(a hinge, a stopper, or can of blue paint).
Sometimes in open moments,
prairie views of ourselves,
we, too, would be on all fours
living our thoughts, trying
the tractor, doll, truck.
Instead, we only trace brief finger
lines along the gaudy boxes
(if we are alone)
and collect the hinge, the stopper,
can of blue paint.
If not fully alive,
we are, at least,
not misunderstood.

THE HUNTER

Did you hear his defense?
His reasoned plea?
"They would die of starvation
if we did not hunt.
We keep them from the
pain, the agony
of cold winter death,"
he says.

Show me one hunter
who kills not
for the kill itself.
Show me one hunter who
rises at dawn to comb the battled fields,
to stalk the forest ridge
till scent and leap and cry —
for mercy's sake alone.

Show me one.

THE POOL AT CORPUS CHRISTI

They threw in seven redwood lounges,
four chairs, and two tables
during the night
(at the diving board end).
The Holiday Inn management had
no explanation, the
workers muttering, "Damn fool kids."
More invectives came as the
clean up finished,
women impatient for their
morning water worship.

Were the kids staying at the Inn
or were they others —
from the city?
Were they peering out from
glassy family rooms ringing the water
or were they
in endless, ragged streets,
their feet in gutter pools?

That would make a difference.

RADIO PREACHER

Raging, he showers
the message of damnation,
red fire, writhing forms;
the car radio vibrating to his
seminary cadence
(the same pauses, the same rise
and fall
and shriek
of voice;
the trained modulations).
Whoever said the Master
raged in such strained, slick
oratory?
My foot vents on the accelerator
until his storm ends and
in sweetness he invites a
love offering
($10 minimum)
in return for a prayer,
area code hot line to heaven.
I think of money changers in the temple,
of Ethan Brand, of the
hypnotist,
of Speech 100,
of the sloganeer, of name brands
and—much later—
in the quiet thought
of love
I know I must embrace this
misguided one
as fully as
I do you.

TURTLE

Raccoon carcass and rigid possum
no longer probing highways. I have seen;
and dogs, of course, jagged corpses.
Rabbits molded into turnpike by Goodyear
as ruts are patched.

I dislike this,
yet in distasteful contrasts
accelerating against remnants unmoving
we are made wise
and motion lured my eyes
on river road. No Mississippi current
or auto speed,
but this dim visage ahead, midway
in four lanes;
it becomes a turtle, six inches of shell
in breadth
in ponderous cadence.
I stop; we meet, his neck unwinding
from secret recess,
and confused, yet knowing, he turns away
as drivers behind me look
with disdain.

Frivolous act!

From them, not him, I move, my last view
indelible of him starting back
in face of traffic, head searching,
eyes high, wide feet thrusting against man.

He looks at me again. I shall
not forget his eyes.
he does not belong there on August concrete.

To comprehend it is to shun his heritage
and, driving on, like some sage
I knew his odds and wept alone.
His shell or cadence I have not known.
That slimy recess, that scaly skin —
this are things that are not akin
to my own ways; yet I am wise
remembering now his high set eyes
which searched for some vain, hopeful clue,
unaware of roadside residue
but sensing danger, seeking home
he plodded. It was like some poem
leading to an awesome theme,
word by step in saddened scheme.
I could have saved him, I watched his head,
but concerned with impatience of cars instead
I left him, and now I thrust
my thoughts out warily, I must
beat again the traffic flow
and raise *my* head, for I know
few would understand these ties,
yet I am linked to him, his eyes
in that moment hunted love.

I cannot find myself above
that call, not in any guise.
I cannot now forget his eyes.

OLD WOMAN

Her hand showed network
of veins,
abundant as the wire mesh
of cart
she dragged along
the narrow walk
while mouthing conversation to herself.
I will avoid this;
she is no part of me.
She stared in antique store window
looking at dusty book, the crooked table,
faded chair and ottoman —
seeing nothing but herself.
Jolting again, she
approached me;
I would have chosen the street,
but race of cars kept me near;
I could feel the ragged membrane of
her coat
as we passed;
a contagion,
plague.
Frantic, I sought to brush it off,
every vistage of the touch of this
old-woman dirt;
and sweep of arm drew me to my own
hand,
to my own veins,
more than I had ever noticed
before.

BOSTON YMCA CHAIR
CARRYING COLOR TAG "ALAMO TANGERINE"

Vestige rare from out the past,
remnant coveted of glory-filled scene
here how to illumine dark hotel room,
Alamo tangerine.
I run fingers over its surface;
charge of horses! sensed in its sheen;
lowring of cattle, cries of harsh battle,
emerging in tangerine.
Arrow pierced its shallow fabric,
this rip in its winding seam
gives evidence of struggle intense
in Alamo tangerine.
Dented arm speaks mute tribute
to hatchet thrown with a scream;
attack on the hill preserved now — and still
in Alamo tangerine.
What liberating thought we have here!
Every struggle on which we can lean
opens wide our thought and whatever we've got
it's in Alamo tangerine.
This table in Boston Tea Party brown
next to Saigon tan desk lamp is seen;
Gettysburg blue walls all over the halls
reflect Alamo tangerine.
San Juan yellow drapes
with wastebasket in Bunker Hill green;
the bathroom sink in Battle of the Bulge pink
blending with tangerine.
Why, the ceiling is in Corregidor white,
the TV has Okinawa gray screen;
colorful bedspread in Pearl Harbor red,
mixing with tangerine.
My gratitude for hotel decor now abounds;
surely you grasp what I mean:
in all history we share, given one YMCA chair
in Alamo tangerine.

MY FATHER'S BIRTHPLACE

Beyond the fields warping,
their green lace
smoothing
in Juneswells,
you see
pines, giant green arrowheads
thrusting skyward.
Enveloped in these sentries
the cool manse lives
unchanged,
and the windowed, single
turret cone
knows of dominion
even as my heart does
each time
I near this
loved place.

WILD RHUBARB

For all this consuming calculus of mine —
bridge girders, Picasso, steam design,
principles of math, Boeing 747,
United Nations and the stars of heaven,
General Motors, throughway sign —
all man's schooling has been mine.
Yet silent, lone, without textbook plan
one day these leaves stretched forth their span,
yawned, and opened to the sun.
Infinitismal tremor, once begun,
spread wise, smiling, even though
I in my wisdom did not know.

REMEMBRANCE

There was Richard in World War Two and
we were
high schoolers together
and he has been gone a generation
and more.
It was a B-17 and it was 1942
and he did not want to go.
I wanted to go, but they took two inches
out of my hip when I was six.
He wanted debate team and school paper
and scholar's books
but there are ten men in a Flying Fortress
and they march with songs of
the wild blue yonder,
like teams bursting through
stadium tunnel,
hearts high as goal posts
and the B-17 opens its insides and
they become part.
"Gear switch."
"Neutral."
"Turbos."
"Off."
"Cabin heat."
"Ready."
"Starting engines!"
Engines alive and you feel spine prickles
and the plane is a living thing and you are
a part of it and a pelican is not meant
to stand always on weathered posts
jutting at water's edge by docks

and a comorant is top heavy and awkward on soil
and the eagle is in cumbersome swagger
at roadside
but when these go aloft
rightness comes
and now you are going to be right and you
say, "Brakes."
"Open."
"Trim tabs."
"Set."
"Generators."
"Checked."
And the throttle moves and the bird moves
and I have known this young man in study
hall, who did not want to fly
and I did want to fly
and I memorized every part
of the B-17
(and the language)
but Richard flew it, not I,
over Italy,
dropping eggs
and it was shot down in a February
splintered wing, rudderless, crippled bird
agonizing,
vomiting ten crew men in wasted residue
and I knew his death
even as I knew my own.
His came flying this bird-plane in clouds
aloft, in flight;
and mine came in emptiness of soil
and in weathered post
and still in cumbersome swagger.

SPRING

No, I'll not write of spring
(I was ready when my trained self
interposed).
It's been done so often with buds
and blossoms
and fresh starts and meadows
and streams.
I will write of a neighbor
or a clock or a loved one
or coincidences
or precisions or something
very profound
like geometry
(lasting poems come from such).

And as I debated this better way —
at that very time, mind you —
with clockwork precision, spring,
like some loved neighbor,
came angling into my room.

There is something to be learned
from such a thing.

MANHOOD

Obese tires toe the mark,
ready to trundle the blazoned
buggy at his whim
and above, in the driver's perch,
eyes steeled in conquest,
he moves fingers along the stick shift,
fondling power as horses piston-kick.
On sidewalks, one talks of groceries,
another pulls dandelions,
and an 8-year-old pushes a plastic truck
up an anthill.
Ordinary afternoon quiet
until one lane opens briefly
and the sputtered Detroit growl
squeezes into merciless howls
and, startled, the car vaults.
He pushes down unseen goggles,
pushes foot on pedal shovel
in power lust.
Tires leave their skin in sudden twin
lanes, and he clutches, lurches,
catapaults,
sling shots himself
for four seconds.
Reality closes in with black lanes
screaming dual protest.
Traffic resumes and one asks,
"Why did he do that?"
Inside, he fondles the shift again and
lifts goggles.
And the little boy goes "vrrooom" with
his plastic truck and giggles
when it makes tracks
on the anthill.

TWO PICTURES FROM POMPEII

I

"Approaching next, on your left the
classic ruins of
the Temple of Jupiter
with remnants of the
public meeting area."
He put the guidebook away;
"Better move along, Martha."
Next, fishing out camera
from enormous bag
he adds,
"Sure looks old, huh? Over
there, Martha! Now, smile —
the bus is waiting."
Such talk for marble clusters,
timeless drapery
for her quick
and meaningless face!

AT THE FORUM

II

"Get away from
that pillar, Henry
it looks like
it'll fall over
any minute."

MEETING THE LECTURER

She burst into early morning
laughter,
alighting from the train,
looking upwards:
"There's my sun!
It followed me through
the night as I knew it would."

She claimed it as her own
and I asked,
"What if there had been clouds?"

"What indeed," she said;
"they never alter truth."

And I followed
this wise person
who knew faith
unshaken by mists.

BLEMISH ON THE
MEMORIAL HALL PLAQUE

Of no meaning, those
years and lives; so long ago.
On the bronze, wall-length
tablet
"In Memoriam, World War I"
in campus building,
judgment now with wads of gum
sticking on "James Miller"
(the "a", the "M", and the "r").

In and out people move,
untouched by this mute
indignity,
this newer death.

PUPPY

"What's the puppy's name?"
I asked the boy on bike,
the gray-white fluff, grinning, in
cardboard box
astride the front wheel.

Dogs have grins so imperceptible
that when one *is* seen
you know you have something
authentic.

"Christmas," the boy said.

"Like a present every day,"
I told myself, and watched them ride away.

FLORIDA

The sun probed autumn clouds
along the ocean
as I, strolling,
surveyed the
causeway's costly homes.
I saw the man
on back steps. He
had a cigar, drew it in, and
held a bottle tightly at
5:30 on a Friday afternoon. He
did not notice me,
nor (more important) the sun,
nor the clouds,
perhaps not even the smoke or drink.
His thoughts, distant, were beyond
my grasp,
but his desolation in my view as close as
his front yard waves
that return and return and return
yet never find a home.

intrigues

GAPS

Time passes
like wisps of clouds
across the face of the moon
and
only occasional gaps
make awareness
of backwards and forwards
and
you wonder
what it would mean
if
there were
no clouds
at all.

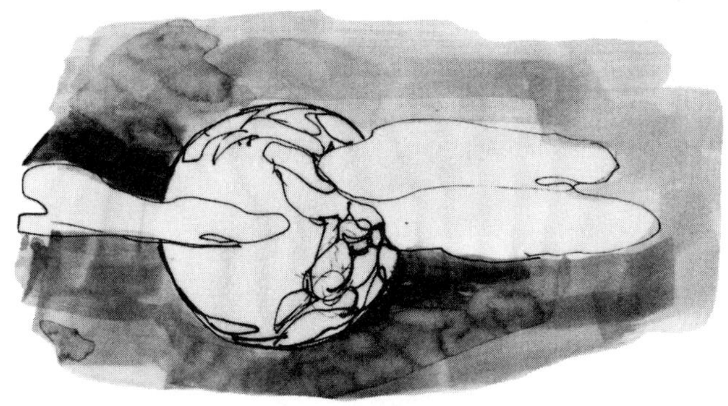

ON THE NATURAL DEATH OF BIRDS

Do the small talons merely
arc slowly,
leaving brief lines
against the limbs
before the plummet
to oblivion?
Or is it bare forkings
in settled dirt —
merely a slow cadence
into leafed burial,
soft closing?
Is this how the lofty bird dies?

Rapid eyes cutting through
green leaf bosom of trees,
then the confident
pulsing
of dominion again:
oh, I have seen them!
Scoriating skies in
thrusted beauty!

But what of the final moment,
the ended flight?
Last burst of wind and wing?

GULF PORT DOCK SCENE

At dockside they align;
scows, trawlers, one-man ships
as rope ladders, masts, shrouds
blend in my panorama
sighted through the clutter.
The *names* stand out.
Mary Ann.
Katie.
Donna Rae.
All of these women
and I wonder what
affection, moment, span
prompted this fisher-boat array
of women's names
and what
Gloria Steinem would have to say.

TO OUR OLD ELECTRIC MIXER

I like the clatter
of the batter
in the beater;
though it's neater
if the latter
doesn't splatter,
yet the pounding
of its sounding
though it's frightful
is delightful
for the clutter
of the butter
in the beater
is much better
than the clitter
of a fritter
getting fatter
in its batter
when the matter
in the beater
finds my platter.

Who can utter
words to flatter
better than a beater?

What is sweeter
for an eater
but the chatter
of the batter
in the beater?

EYELID

Beneath my eyelid
these patterns, like kaleidoscopes
that are at once a murky blend,
then lines
that aggregate, and at certain
fleeting times
(looking at the sun will help)
they are dots,
Rohrshachs,
impatient little blobs that
veer off the edge
when I try to focus.
I think of close-up photography,
those full pages in old Life magazines
of cellular structure
and wonder if
I am seeing the stuff
of what I am, in these
under-eyelid pastorals.

TESSERACT

(Theoretical four-dimensional figure)

The tesseract,
so purely logical,
raises issue.
If two points
make a line,
four lines a square,
six squares define a cube —
then, one is told,
eight cubes establish
the tesseract, enclosing,
defining.
I have the logic, yet
cannot view this, nor accept.
But I do know of a child's love,
dispelling rancor;
my brother's smile, lofting my heart,
hands enfolding where distance
once ruled:
from these, assurance
that others,
pyramiding love,
will establish, define
without limit.
I will hold to these.

Perhaps I will
return to the
tesseract
some other day.

CEMETERY REGULATIONS, MEMORIAL DAY

"All flowers must be in metal containers" —
so let there be no complainers —
"removed by Tuesday noon, a must."
And so we all, consigned to dust,
will await these tributes in stated hours.
The grounds crewmen would cut the flowers
in wide swaths if left another day.
Distasteful, but there's no better way
to keep Happy Acres manicured,
earth rest efficiently secured.
And let there be no tombstones
to mark the site of wasting bones;
they would interfere with maintenance
tractor mowers some days hence.

This surface-based economy,
this bland scene appeals not to me.
Those beneath, in residue,
heeded not this point of view.
In life, untidy, they left heel marks,
spilled their drinks, cluttered parks,
scratched the car, in design defamed,
let weeds and daisies sprout untamed,
and building homes or families,
or painting rooms, or planting trees
created little monuments.
We treasure now each evidence.

This cemetery, flat, sterile, shaven,
reflects not a proper haven
for our lifetime flowers, wildly growing;
it perpetuates only efficient mowing.

WHO DECIDES?

You've seen them?
Rippling blankets,
clusters of birds
that from their forages
unison to the air in
vibrant, communal sweeps?
How is the leader known?
What mystique of call decides?

The morning moves over me.
What is known, what I touch,
I understand.

Only what is known,
only what I touch.

WINTER AFTERNOON

Fingertip trees
thrust from
white lace ground.
Across
deepless, metal sky
lone bird
slides.

Silver stream
carries
ice wafers
in languid journey
at rim of day,
etching
February.

COLORADO STREAM

Its purpose clearer than
the bright boulder-probed transparency
which lures your eye from highway,
this stream writhes willingly,
tumbling cold,
yet in watery abandon.
Where? Where?
Losing sight of cars, never of purpose,
always one goal, gravity defined
for each drop;
each turn bringing closer
the seas where all waters gather.
Oceanic meeting house.
Purpose met.
Hurry! Hurry!
I watch from berm of road
and question,
Where is the ocean of my purpose?
Am I as willing to tumble and turn
to find it?

QUIET SANDALS

And love
in quiet sandals moves about,
stopping in deep moments
when we find each other.

Twos.
We revere twos,
one with one;
two fingers uplifted,
two hands entwined
(especially if yours and mine).

But if quiet sandals move on past —
the ones, still ones, now in contrast
wonder, is there the moment when
they will turn to us again?

TEMPERING

The gull along the restless shore
stood on one leg; I saw no more.
What had prompted such a stance?
He moved then, in a kind of dance
that was no pose for other birds,
his look at me was beyond words;
smug, he slowly unwound his limb —
it jacknifed in poetic hymn
that suggested joy to me
and more — it was his victory.
I suspect now my point is made:
in all my time to promenade
I could never retract, tuck a leg in
under my wrinkled stomach skin.
He was beyond me; as it unwound
I merely watched, and then I frowned
and as he sauntered off on two
I heard him laugh; well, such things accrue—
there is a tempering in being aware
through the things we see, the things we bear.

TEXAS FROM
AMERICAN AIRLINES

From 30,000 feet
the dry river beds, the
brief canyons,
are forkings,
dark sprays against the canvas.

You think of leaf-stems
petrified in rock,
wispy traces
in the same design.

Beauty perseveres
close, far.

interpretations

PICTURE OF A
STARVING CHILD

No, I have not seen the
children, just pictures:
the war orphans,
the little hands reaching,
the desperate faces
of those outcast,
the crying babe mid the shelled
streets, the naked girl
fleeing napalm.
And
this starving one, the buttock-boy
astride some nameless, dirty road
in India, bones of legs askew,
his pitiful threads of arms
between,
propping the listless
oversize head.
Burden of skull
beyond the tragic arms.
What did he with camera do?
Lens rewards this moment
but I know—
so deeply etched within me the knowing —
beyond the distillation
of the photograph
the pitiful head moves closer
to the dirt.
I know it moves,
its last journey
defined in the
unfulfilled dream
that the child never knew
he had.

TEACHER

Lives, not mere faces,
are in
classroom rows,
though impatience,
despair, sullen view
interposing
would have this
unremembered.
Chalkboards express disciplines
in hourly cadence.
Teachers show remembrances.

FACES

Faces
(toads, angels, stars, weeds).
We seek to interpret them,
forgetting
that
minds loom behind them
(child, aged, busy, untouched).
Faces are easier.

THE WIND

Tattler!

You feel you must
run ahead, spreading news
of rain, ice, darkness, dust.

Gossip!

Bending tree ears, telling this
and making limbs agog
in frenzied synthesis.

Tale bearer!

Hustling clouds, setting them askew,
then banging on our doors.
Just can't wait, can you?
No secrets with you around,
rushing in pell mell;
if I had any news
you'd be the *last* I would tell.

PROCESSION

In the early morning slate air
at the Nebraska farm
black steer glisten,
unwinding in long procession.
They weave in obedient lines
toward pasture, rhythmic time
of hoof, nose, trunk in slow rolls.
I think of parades
and school children
returning from recess,
and political parties,
of circus entrances,
elephant walk,
red ants,
whistle of steel mill,
and of
families.

JUDD HOUSE

Antietam's rage, but a decade past, heard
when from the dusty lane I stirred
and thrust myself against a summer sky.
I came from tree, from clay, from soil,
from one man's vision and the toil
of the workmen lofted high
on beams which weaved a home for students:
hotel, Judd House, the campus Inn.

You were unborn when I knew my century begin.
Straight boards laced me tightly,
holding upright more than form, my proud years
in ripening time; and since
I became the college, I've housed its
presidents.

Not wind nor pace of trucks
nor winter's rage nor some devil's deed —
my rubbled death is not of these.
But of time, and of need
that led to the iron ball
that led to the jarring fall
and tractor's corrugated lines
across my dusty bones
before there came the summer sky.
Tell again now of my birth,
remember now my birth.
Trace again now my straight boards,
remember now my boards.
Close now in quiet thought my rooms,
remember now my rooms.
Walk again my narrow steps,
remember now my steps.

Hold the voices of the past,
remember now my past.
Know the touch of your grandfather's hand,
know the warmth of memories
as I have known a century's.

Remember me when summer sky returns.

Remember me.

Remember me.

PEDAGOGUE

Ipso facto and *sina quo non* and thus and so *cum laude;*
I consider myself an authority on *op cit*
as well.
Magnum opus and *ergo*
go nicely with *et al* as well.
If A then not B
ergo.
Proviso and compendium and let it be known
ipso facto magna cum note card
it is *per quod* because *ergo* is *ergo.*
Ah! A square ergo!
Hypotenuse, Decartes, Pythagoras, factotum
and when in the course
of human events it becomes
necessary
that unless and wherefore
it is not to be unconsidered
inconsequential
ibid ibid ibid
ibid ibid
ibid.

FLYING MODEL AIRPLANES

Counting was important.
Some took 75 turns,
others as many as 500,
set by bulkheads, stringers,
type of rubber band.
I held the fuselage
and looked in the cockpit eye,
dreaming of rubber pedals,
and bank indicators, RPM,
as I cranked the balsa propeller,
felt it tighten
against my forefinger.

Each turn I gave
meant one more upward
leap
for the model airplane
and, just as well,
for the sky-filled realm
of my heart.

SQUIRREL AND TAIL

Duty? Perhaps it was
as they moved across the lawn
towards some purpose beyond my view.

It was the sequence I absorbed:
one gray squirrel, yet two in flight
for his body-long duster tail, not upright
nor arrowed
was coursing in slow arcs
with each lope — spring, hurtle, descent —
patterning exactly the
body sweep
and, so, two curves.

Sequential harmony.

Duty? Or was it structure?

But a jet's contrails are of different
substance,
a cat's tail is liks a flag,
the wake of boat hunts shore on
either side,
and a mouse merely drags his.
Was it habit?
This rhythmical, squirrel-tail curve?
Like a child playing house

imitating the elder body
it was
and I followed
both in each,
this cadenced undulating.

Now, recalling the beauty of
the parent leap
I say perhaps it was
neither duty
nor habit
nor yet structure
that spurred this
dual ribboning.

Perhaps
it was admiration.

PELICAN

On constant winds he sweeps
across white sand manor
at water's edge,
splits silent currents
with long beak prow,
then with lancet wings
that end in fringe.
Pulsing wings,
he descends to ocean's peak,
beauty of the flight
acknowledged
in surfaced offerings
and in cadenced clapping
of the waves.

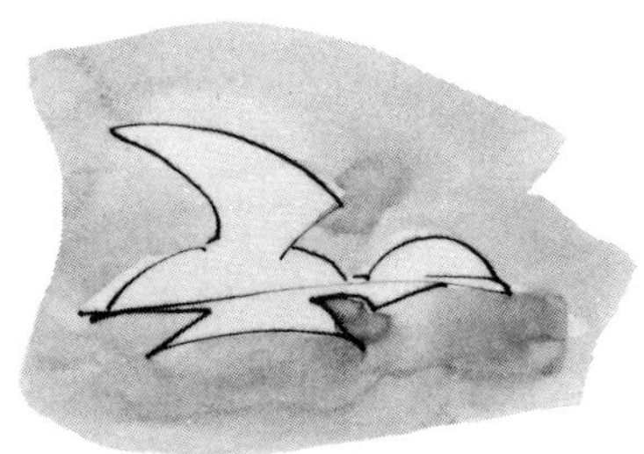

SLUMS, PHILADELPHIA SUBURB

From motion
they are acceptable,
merely
corrugating brotherly hillsides.

These houses are
best in turnpike blurs,
for I am uncomfortable
when I focus
on them,
these human shambles
scarring pitiful slopes.

There is
comfort
in motion.

TRUTH

Openings that fling
or only separate
but open;
woodpile crevices for mice to
disappear into;
doorways in and out,
shutters of our minds,
precise lenses, tree borings,
and mortar cracks,
slivers of light
confirming;
gauze partings
telling.
We seek these
patches that freshen
in
wisps
of affirmations,
instant glimpses,
tellings,
unhinged moments,
visions of what is
that persist
after they
pass through,
hurrying on
to the universalities
we know of
only
through them.

KANSAS DUSK

With the quilt of Kansas
on either side of road,
alone, I weave a quiet journey;
see the sheen of obedient cattle
lining home from forage
in the duskglow,
the first star opening.
I see the proud silhouettes
of thrusting silos,
see the dip and roll of land
fade as night appears.
I have not known these before,
yet each around — the field,
the herd, the farm —
bring remembrance of other times.

We link all to ourselves
in discerning what these are;
beauty, design, duty,
in field, in farm, in star.

READING POEMS

Reading poems for understanding
even aloud and
in studious need
we may find differences
of opinion.
It is like
you and I
being touched by the motion of the wind
across our faces
for unless our eyes are tuned,
our checks aligned,
nostrils exact
in catching the single current,
interpretations come.
Our faces are not one.
Yet winds need not distress;
for later
when the bird is silent
and the work of the breeze
is seen in tufts of leaves
and in settled lines
of dust against the window,
we talk about the wafted impress,
dimensions of the touch,
and find our heart's response.

It is then
we understand
the
differences.

POINT OF VIEW

This young polka-dot robin
that paused on green rim of stone bath
deciding, head cocked in searching
did not know how much I hoped.
For him it was cleansing ritual considered,
but my moment hung as I waited
and watched his eyes as he debated.
Then he plunged
and I reveled in his ordered ways;
beak under, then forward thrust, and up
and on to rim, the preening, layering back
the folds, feather engines whirring.

What was this affirmation? You may ask:
for him it was merely a needful task
of body, made in routine measure;
for me it was insight, knowledge, pleasure.

JUNE LAUNDROMAT

The city has been scrubbed tonight,
washed twice, then rinsed well
and tumbled by persistent winds
from the west
after the electricity went off
and little children could go to sleep
unafraid.
Glistening now in the rain sheen,
trees show branches undefined
in pallid, dry grayness, and
thick gumbo soup of leaves
floats in trenches by the road, touring
drainpipes under driveways
when walks shout at you under street lights
clean, so clean when you walk your dog
and his legs get stringy wet you won't mind
him in the house afterwards.
Your own shoes show mottled wetness
but it will pass.
Clean, scrubbed night, and above
blowing restlessly away
are the lint clouds.
Automatic washing
every spring.

GETTING DOWN IN WEEDS

It's a right thing,
getting down in weeds
that catapault skyward
on their own
in vacant city lots
every summer.
Scraunch.
That's the word.
I'm not sure how to spell it
but I know what it means.
With your chin on the ground
the wind-swept fabric
of wild mustard or foxtail grass
is taller than the new bank
or the hamburger shack
or the Texaco sign.

And the point is
that
may really be the truth.

JUNIOR HIGH

Thirteen, perhaps; he pauses with
studied manner
out of NBC, pulls a filter king from
rain jacket, lets it suspend
from pursed lips
dried by autumn winds.
It is seven forty-five;
junior high home room soon.
Blue shirt, tail out, tight chinos,
uncombed hair, meager lunch held loosely,
he leans forward,
draws ashes into the filter king
till my countdown ends
(I am in the car at the light, reading
the intersection)
and ignition completes this
public coupling.
Then he becomes another early morning
chimney
along with U.S. Steel.
Flicking, then hunching,
he walks on,
inhaling visions of all the tablet of manhood:
conquest, adoration, virility, ease.
Visions against a cold, blue morning.
Pulp paper targets along the rifle range.

BUTTERFLY

Dancing first.
Not fluttering, however much
it has been said.
Dancing.
There are, of course,
other accomplishments:
they may appear as nothing more
than aimless flag-flitting
but there is
placing,
testing,
nimble, hesitant wingtip touchings,
antennae ferretings,
monarchial musings,
and wispy leg clutchings.
First, though,
dancing.

PROF AND STUDENT

Have you ever seen a prof
when his dignity is off?
With his classroom air all shot
now that everything's been taught?
Shoes off, bad joke, peanut butter,
evening paper, crazy dreams, fix the shutter,
television, Saturday bath, atom bomb,
Dr. Pepper, bank book balance, note to Mom,
chase the dog, clean your room, many meetings,
on the phone, off to church, and Christmas greetings,
cheese sandwich, love, pleased, and worried,
ping pong, model cars, and always hurried,
heartaches, glories, bit of fame:
prof or student — much the same.

MOVING

And so time moves on
in little globules, glass sacs
of moments
like snow scenes in a
transparent ball.

I pick one up
and hold it in my hand,
shake my head to stir a scene.
The time I got a Lionel for Christmas.
The time of the dance at Purdue,
the times our children were born.
Moments not lined in a row,
but piled high, jostled, tumbled,
and some, I fear, may already be
beyond my reach.

But I keep shaking my head,
trying.
There is good in trying.

SUNDAY MORNING

Thirty minutes before
Sunday School
I reached up,
coupling mind and hand,
to implant a new bulb
in ceiling fixture
above our table.
At that moment, I heard,
in jest,
"Quite unusual for a teacher!"

We laughed,
but, later, during class,
I found it novel not at all.
Mid books, discussion,
we were *all*
reaching,
implanting light,
truth.

POETRY

"Hello, words!"
I said, opening the
doors, settling back against
the cushioned chair.
"I've been thinking
about you;
wanting to talk.
What do you have this time?"

My friends responded
in lines that bristled across
the windows of their rooms
with insights and tales
and curiosities
and discoveries.

Never a sameness, even if
the doors are worn with use;
inside, the words,
deepening with meaning,
give fresh views
each time
I enter.

APPLE PARINGS

It is expression; that's what we are —
a moment, a memory, a falling star
of recallings and sharings.
I've given you some apple parings
of my mind: dogs in cars, aspen leaves,
honeymooners, tesseract, old man who grieves,
a turtle, chair, some clouds, Pompeii,
a bird in song before the day,
pup named Squirt, a building's quiet halls,
Kansas steer, squirrel, gaunt child who falls,
the prof in class, and hands that enfold,
a mixer, hairpiece, springtime, and a marigold,
man of rainbows, B-17, a motel pool,
model airplanes, family, last visit to my school.

One man's runaway thought, in expression endures —
for all these were mine, and now they are **yours.**

Lyle Crist teaches creative writing, literature, and journalism at Mount Union College in Alliance, Ohio. His light-hearted programs on language and communication have won plaudits from audiences throughout the United States. His previous books include *Man Expressed: The Realm of Writing* (Macmillan-Glencoe) and *Through the Rain and Rainbow: The Remarkable Life of Richard Kinney* (Abingdon).